Original title:
The Chorus of Cedars

Copyright © 2025 Creative Arts Management OÜ
All rights reserved.

Author: Maya Livingston
ISBN HARDBACK: 978-1-80567-435-1
ISBN PAPERBACK: 978-1-80567-734-5

Lament of the Evergreen Vowels

Oh, the a's and e's take flight,
In branches tall, they sing at night.
The i's grow tired, shift in their seats,
While o's roll round, with no defeat.

A u sneezes, drops a pine,
While vowels dance in joy divine.
But z's, my friend, they seldom show,
Too busy with their woe, oh no!

The Gathering of Pine Cones

Once a cone, so small and round,
Dared to roll from ground to ground.
Chased by squirrels who want a snack,
It dodged and weaved, what a knack!

Pine cones met for a grand feast,
Joked about the worst of beasts.
"Who's the funniest?" one cone said,
"Fallen branches, in their dread!"

Songs beneath the Starry Boughs

Underneath the moonlit leaves,
The critters jam with their knotted sleeves.
A raccoon strums on a shiny tin,
While owls hoot loud, just to join in.

The nightingale pitches in too,
Making sure the beats are true.
Squirrels clap with tiny paws,
Singing loud without a cause!

The Symphony of Swaying Branches

Branches sway in breezy haste,
Concerts start without a taste.
Leaves applaud with a rustling cheer,
While squirrels tap dance, bringing queer.

A tenor crow sings out of tune,
Catcalls echo 'neath the moon.
Nature's fun, a wild delight,
Every night a party, oh what sight!

The Silent Chime of Arboreal Symphony

In the forest, trees do sway,
Their whispers cause leaves to play.
Squirrels dance with acorn grace,
While branches tickle, just in case.

Barking dogs in foolish chase,
Raccoons giggle in their place.
With each creak, a gnarled pun,
Nature's laughter, oh what fun!

The wind joins in, a playful tease,
Turning twigs into giant keys.
Unlocking secrets, rickety rhymes,
Nature's jest in perfect times.

A lumberjack with borrowed hat,
Tripped on roots, a comical spat.
The trees chuckle, oh, what a scene,
Nature's show, where joy is keen.

The Tapestry of Timbered Harmony

Woodland creatures sing a tune,
Beneath the light of a silly moon.
Chipmunks chirp and owls hoot,
Making music in their root.

Branches lend their croaky voice,
In every rustle, there's a choice.
To join the choir, bark on bark,
The tiny critters spark the spark.

Mice on leaves, a tiny stage,
Each act a giggle, every page.
Bouncing badgers, prancing prunes,
The forest floor holds merry tunes.

In the shade, where shadows play,
Laughter echoes, day by day.
The tapestry of wood and air,
Woven with joy, beyond compare.

Celestial Beats of Leaf and Limb

Leaves drop beats like fallen stars,
Dancing troopers join from afar.
Roots in rhythm, trees align,
Nature's concert, a grand design.

Bongs of branches, syncopate,
Each gust of wind, they celebrate.
A twiggy solo, oh so loud,
Under the gaze of the giggly cloud.

Beetles tap and crickets sing,
In this jamboree, life's the king.
Every sound a silly twist,
In this forest, none are missed.

So if you're near, take up the sound,
Join the fun where vibes abound.
In the canopy's embrace so wide,
Funny feelings can't be denied.

Whispers from the Timeless Age

In the woods, a squirrel stares,
With acorns dancing in his lairs.
He complains about the noisy leaves,
And blames them for the tricks up sleeves.

Oh, the trees, they shake and sway,
Laughing at the critters' play.
Each branch bends with a creaky tone,
While mossy cushions make them groan.

Beneath the boughs, a rabbit hops,
In search of carrots and sweet crops.
But lo! A deer with a grand old tale,
Tells him how to ride the gale.

So they gather, all in cheer,
Making friends, year after year.
With whispered jokes, they crack up loud,
In their leafy, silly crowd.

An Ode to the Hushed Grove

In secret nooks where shadows play,
The crickets plan their grand ballet.
They chirp and chirp, a rhythmic beat,
While fireflies twirl on tiny feet.

The owls hoot facts, so wise and bright,
But mostly just complain all night.
"Who cooked those beans?" one sarcastic yells,
Echoing through the scented swells.

The mischievous raccoons, masked and sly,
Steal berries from beneath the sky.
They giggle as they stash their loot,
Planning a party with fruits to boot.

But watch out for the porcupine's quill,
His jokes are sharp and quite a thrill.
In this quiet glen, the laughter grows,
As nature spins her funny shows.

The Forest's Gentle Serenade

The breeze waltzes through the trees,
Teasing branches with playful ease.
A bird's off-key song makes all cringe,
It's no wonder they start to sing.

The mushrooms chuckle, round and spry,
Catching sunlight with a cheeky sigh.
"When do we get to wear a hat?"
They giggle under a large, fat cat.

The stumps are stools for the wise old toad,
He shares secrets down the shady road.
With laughter ringing through the leaves,
Every creature knows, this joy achieves.

In this ballet of laughter free,
Nature's jesters dance in glee.
Together, they'll create a tune,
Till twilight hums a sleepy rune.

Feathered Songs in the Open Sky

A parrot dressed in shiny flair,
Mocks the owl with a feathered stare.
With a wink and twist, he takes to flight,
Writing jokes in the morning light.

The geese waddle, quite unimpressed,
They honk at all who try their best.
"Why fly south when we can jog?"
They strut about like a chatty dog.

In the sun, a lark sings high,
While robins argue 'bout the pie.
"Who took the crust?" they squabble round,
In every branch, the gossip's found.

Cheery whispers fill the air,
While vibrant songs tease without a care.
In this wood, humor freely flows,
As feathered friends trade silly prose.

Hymn of the Hidden Giants

In the woods, they shake and sway,
Old trees giggle, come what may.
Squirrels launch from branch to branch,
Wondering if they'll find romance.

Mossy boots and acorn hats,
Pine cones dance, oh how they chat!
Nature's jesters, wise and spry,
They tickle leaves as breezes sigh.

Dance of the Whispering Cedars

Twisting trunks with clumsy grace,
Tall ones falling in this race.
Roots entwined in playful muck,
'Don't trip over!'... Ah, bad luck!

Branches wave like silly hands,
Inviting all to twist and prance.
Laughter echoes through the green,
As trees waltz, a funny scene.

Voices Linger in the Gloom

Under shadows, whispers grow,
Branches mumble tales we know.
'Hey there, leaf! Why don't you peek?',
'Stop bouncing, twig! You're such a freak!'

In the dark, they share their woes,
'Watch out for that pigeon's toes!'
Giggles weave through thickened air,
As shadows dance without a care.

The Chorus of Resilient Spirits

With every groan, the trunks erupt,
Chirping birds distract, interrupt.
'Hold your boughs! No sleep tonight!'
'Who'll tell jokes? Let's bring the light!'

Roots rumble as they sway along,
Rough and tough, but still so strong.
They shake their leaves, what silly sprites,
Singing loudly, chasing heights.

Echoing Through the Canopy

In the woods, a squirrel squeaks,
Bouncing high between the peaks.
A chatty bird joins in the fray,
It's a raucous, feathery ballet.

The trees sway gently to the beat,
With acorns dancing at their feet.
A chipmunk tries to steal the show,
As the sunlight steals the glow.

The leaves gossip in the breeze,
Sharing secrets with such ease.
What's that rustle? A playful hare,
Stirring laughter in the air.

Beneath the boughs, all join along,
Singing nature's quirky song.
Each critter adding their own tune,
In this woodland, joyful commune.

The Ballad of Woodland Harmony

Once a tree had quite a plan,
To jive with critters, be the man.
But when he started to break dance,
The owls just laughed, didn't give a chance.

A fox performed a little jig,
While a hedgehog tried to grow big.
The dainty fawns, they rolled in mirth,
Turning twirls upon soft earth.

A raccoon brought baked acorn pies,
And joy exploded in the skies.
Who knew the woods held such delight?
As laughter echoed into the night.

A symphony of furry fun,
Their antics shining like the sun.
When nature's crew decides to play,
Mirthful moments steal the day.

Rhapsody of the Leafy Embrace

In the shade of leafy layers,
Lies a troupe of funny players.
A bear dons glasses, reads a book,
While the wise old owl gives a look.

A tree stump hosts the daily quiz,
Where raccoons ponder what is whiz.
"Is that a snack or just a dream?"
They argue with a joyful gleam.

The flowers nod as the winds puff,
Tickling ferns, it's all quite tough.
The butterflies spread silly news,
Of a snail who sported bright blue shoes.

Every leaf has tales to share,
In the laughter of the woodland air.
With giggles sprouting from each root,
Nature's jesters, their funny salute.

Timbered Tranquility

Cedar trees stand tall and grand,
Whispering jokes across the land.
A woodpecker thinks he's a star,
Drumming beats like a rock guitar.

Beneath the branches, shadows play,
As critters tumble every day.
A badger stumbles, loses his hat,
With a cheeky grin, he chases a rat.

A rabbit hops with flair, oh my!
Doing ballet as clouds float by.
The wise old tortoise winks with glee,
Laughing softly, "Stay slow like me!"

In this wood, where humor thrives,
All are welcome, the fun arrives.
With nature's giggles in clear tone,
Timbered serenity, all on loan.

The Singing Shells of Earth

In the forest, where whispers play,
Shells gather to gossip the day away.
The breeze tickles leaves in hearty laughter,
Squirrels roll their eyes, chasing after.

One clam grins wide, a secret to share,
While crabs do the cha-cha, without a care.
They tap their toes on the sandy ground,
Nature's dance floor is where laughs abound.

An otter joins in, a slick little lad,
Swings 'round the trees, oh isn't he rad!
With shellfish bands playing tunes so sweet,
All of earth's creatures move to the beat.

Beneath a moonlit, chuckling sky,
Even the snails start to dance and fly.
If you listen close, you might hear their song,
A wacky tune where all of us belong.

Ballad of the Wildwood Spirits

In the glade, spirits swirl and twirl,
With mischief aglow and a wink and a whirl.
They hide in the shadows and peek from the trees,
Making the branches sway with the breeze.

A gnome with a grin, in his pointy hat,
Shares tales of frogs who wear shoes and chat.
The mushrooms are giggling, each one a bard,
Telling wild stories in the backyard.

Fireflies flash as they dance on the air,
While owls drop jokes with a wise little stare.
The spirits pass tips on how to take flight,
While raccoons play cards under soft moonlight.

Together they laugh till the first light appears,
The woods filled with echoes of boisterous cheers.
What a sight to behold in this magical glen,
Where the wildwood spirits are up to again!

Chant Amongst the Bark and Needles

Amidst the trees, a songbirds' choir,
Chirps out jokes that will never tire.
Beneath the boughs, the squirrels perform,
With acorns aplenty, creating a swarm.

One little chipmunk, with a bow on his tail,
Recites poetry, making all hearts sail.
Bark grows a grin, and needles join in,
While laughing leaves rustle, a playful din.

A porcupine plays a wild game of charades,
While critters keep score in leafy cascades.
Their laughter is light, their spirits run high,
As shadows stretch long in the brightening sky.

With each merry chime, the forest comes alive,
In this woodland, it's certain all creatures thrive.
So merry our gathering, beneath the green veil,
For nature's merriment tells the most jolly tale!

The Harmonized Hush of the Forest

The forest hums with a silly tune,
As creatures join in under the moon.
With critters in clusters, a soft serenade,
They strut in the shadows, fearless and unafraid.

A duo of deer, prancing with flair,
Compete in a dance that's beyond compare.
A hedgehog chimes in with a whistle so bright,
Tunes that would wake even the stars of the night.

Owls clap their wings, a rhythmic applause,
While turtles spin tales with their slow, clever jaws.
As whispers emerge from the trees with delight,
The harmonious hush steals away the night.

With laughter and giggles, the woodland unites,
As crickets provide the percussion in flights.
In this forest of giggles, with joy on the rise,
We find solace and laughter beneath starry skies.

Euphony in the Woodlands

In the forest where laughter rings,
Trees wear hats and dance with springs.
Frogs croak jokes, so bright and bold,
With leaves that giggle, stories told.

Squirrels chatter with little flair,
While branches shake without a care.
The sun's a jester, flipping rays,
Tickling trunks in playful ways.

Mice weave tales in leafy beds,
Of acorns growing funny heads.
The owls hoot wisdom, wise yet sly,
As wind whispers, "Let's all try!"

Nature's choir sings fun and cheer,
In a world of giggles, we revere.
So join the jest in leafy halls,
Where every creature shares their calls.

In the Shadow of the Pinewood Choir

Beneath the pines, a tune does play,
Where shadows sway and critters stay.
A raccoon strums a twig-made lute,
While chipmunks jiggle in their boots.

The wind's the drummer, tapping beats,
As hedgehogs shuffle on tiny feet.
Joyful whispers fill the air,
With pinecones tossed without a care.

An owl with spectacles reads the score,
While beavers tap dance by the shore.
Every note a playful wink,
In woodlands where we pause and think.

Yet even trees have something grand,
Their branches raise a merry hand.
With laughter loud, they lift the night,
In shadows where the joy takes flight.

Ode to the Living Monuments

Oh, towering trunks with smiles so wide,
Guardians of laughter, side by side.
Bark chuckles softly, wrapped in grace,
While critters frolic in leafy space.

Whispers echo from roots to sky,
"Watch out for squirrels, they might fly!"
Branches twist in playful jest,
Where every breeze feels like a fest.

Each ring a story, each leaf a joke,
With every rustle, the branches poke.
To nature's jesters, we must raise,
A toast of joy in leafy praise!

So let us dance beneath their boughs,
Join in the laughter, take our vows.
For in this grove, so lush and true,
The living giants play, it's all for you.

The Lilt of Lush Life

In gardens lush where giggles bloom,
Flowers tell tales that lift the gloom.
A daisy's wink, a tulip's twist,
In nature's laugh, we can't resist.

Butterflies flutter with silly grace,
Dipping low, a whimsical race.
While bees hum tunes in busy throngs,
Creating rhythm where life belongs.

The wind jokes softly, whispers sweet,
As jolly vines embrace our feet.
In this dance of lively light,
Every leaf knows how to ignite.

So join the flora, spread your cheer,
In this bustling world, hold it dear.
For in the lilt of every sigh,
The fun of life will always fly.

Rhapsody in the Woodland Silence

In the woods where squirrels prance,
Trees wear hats—what a chance!
Bark-patterned coats, all in line,
Cackling bugs sip sweet sunshine.

The owls throw shade, quite the scene,
While chipmunks dance, oh so keen.
Acorns drop with comedic thuds,
As foxes laugh in leafy buds.

Beneath the pines, the raccoons joke,
Planning mischief with each poke.
Branches swaying in a jig,
Nature's stage, big and big!

The breeze brings giggles, light and free,
As critters play hide-and-seek with glee.
Rooted spouses, evergreen glares,
Nature's laughter fills the flares.

Hymn of the Whispering Pines

In the pines, a gossip flies,
The squirrels roll their winking eyes.
"Did you hear the woodpecker's crime?
He's drilling holes just for a rhyme!"

With whispers soft, the trees convene,
A council made of every green.
"Let's prank the humans at the park,
And leave them wondering till it's dark!"

Branches swing like lopsided chairs,
As birds compose their wild affairs.
The laughter rustles in the leaves,
Nature's humor—oh, how it weaves!

As sunlight dapples, shadows peek,
A badger tries to hide, yet squeaks.
With every gust, the forest chuckles,
Nature's jokes bring giggly buckles.

Murmurs of Nature's Guardians

In ancient groves where secrets swell,
The elder trees begin to tell,
Of lumberjacks who lost their way,
While trying to chop for a bouquet!

Mighty sentinels stand so tall,
With vines that wrap like a cozy shawl.
"Those hikers think they're so profound,
But we've seen them trip on solid ground!"

Leaves chuckle when the storms arise,
As rain kicks dust in fell disguise.
The roots will snicker, come what may,
Invisible giggles come to play.

Crickets serenade the stars,
While toads debate their roles as "farce."
In whispered tones, they share their schemes,
Nature's hilarity flows in dreams.

Ode to the Stalwart Sentinels

Stalwart giants clad in green,
Guardians of the woodland scene.
With every breeze, they tease and jest,
Mocking shadows, they're truly blessed.

At twilight hours, the wolves come near,
The trees watch closely, full of cheer.
"Let's start a band!" the branches sigh,
And sing until the stars run dry!

Twirling vines and creeping moss,
Nature knows neither gain nor loss.
"Did you hear about the skunk?" one said,
"His perfume scares off thieves in bed!"

With hearty chuckles, the forest glows,
Filling the air where the wild wind blows.
From root to crown, above and below,
Nature's merriment steals the show.

Lament of the Lost Canopy

Oh, where have the leaves all gone?
My hat's a perfect lawn!
Squirrels dance, but I trip
On twigs during my skip.

The trees all laugh, it seems,
As I chase my wild dreams.
"Grow up!" they shout with glee,
But who are they, not me?

Old branches gossip and sigh,
"Remember when we were spry?"
But now they creak and moan,
While I'm here all alone.

A lost canopy, what a scene,
It's a forest of feline cuisine!
Cats chase leaves; what a show,
Should I laugh or just go slow?

The Ethereal Song of the Green Giants

In the woods, they sing so loud,
The giants all gather proud.
With voices thick as bark,
They hum till it's dark.

They try to dance - it's a sight,
Tripping on roots left and right.
"Who stepped on my foot?" they bellow,
Leaving a trail of green fellows.

The moon peeks through their limbs,
As they tune their funny hymns.
All while I grab my snack,
Hiding laughter at their knack.

Up high, their giggles soar,
Bouncing off forest floor.
It's an operatic tease,
With nature's rustling breeze.

Whispers of the Wooded Sanctuary

In the glade, the whispers play,
As nature chats the day away.
"Why did the tree cross the road?"
"To leaf behind its heavy load!"

The bushes chuckle in delight,
While tall oaks flex with all their might.
"Do trees ever have fun?" they ask,
"It's a limb-pressive task!"

A troll hides beneath the bridge,
Trying hard not to fidget.
"Why so serious? Lighten up!"
They're brewing mischief in a cup.

The sanctuary's alive with cheer,
With every joke that's crystal clear.
Join the forest's playful spree,
Where laughter's as tall as the trees!

The Gathering of Sylvan Souls

The souls of woodlands unite today,
For a quirky, leafy ballet.
"Who stole my acorn pie?" they shout,
As little critters run about.

Moss carpets the little stage,
While the trees turn over a new page.
"Let's hear your best jokes!" they cheer,
"Nothing's funnier than a deer!"

As shadows flicker and sway,
A hedgehog joins the fray.
With quirky puns from the ground,
The best woodland humor is found!

In this space, they twirl and spin,
Laughter echoes; let the fun begin!
Nature's laughter fills the air,
In this gathering, joy we share.

Cadence of the Woodland Spirits

In the woods, the spirits sing,
Squirrels dance, and robins swing.
Acorns fall with silly plinks,
Nature's laughter, oh, it stinks!

Trees wear hats made of bright moss,
While ferns gossip, never cross.
Mushrooms giggle in a row,
Giving secrets to the crow.

Fairies trip on tiny toes,
While bees boast of who they chose.
A raccoon wears a festive tie,
Interpreting the clouds up high.

A deer prances, makes a bet,
Will the fox remember yet?
With all the jesters of the grove,
Nature's whimsy shines and roves.

Resonance of Root and Sky

Roots are tangled in a chase,
Laughter echoes, full of grace.
The trees gossip, sway and tease,
While squirrels plot to steal the cheese.

Clouds drift by in a fuzzy race,
Winds whistle tunes, a funny bass.
A parrot squawks in comic tones,
Making jokes with falling stones.

Foxes huddle, sharing tales,
Of wobbly owls and sneezy snails.
A badger hums a droll refrain,
As laughter dances through the grain.

The sun peeks in with a wink,
While rivers giggle, splash, and clink.
In this space of joy galore,
Nature's humor we adore.

Tales of the Verdant Watchers

Mighty guardians, green and tall,
Watch the antics, catch the fall.
Branches wave, and shadows play,
In this forest, fun's the way!

Ladybugs wear coats of red,
Bold imaginations fed.
Grasshoppers leap with comic grace,
As butterflies race in their place.

The owls, wise with piercing stares,
Chuckle softly, spread their flares.
While rabbits snicker, hide and seek,
In the dusk, their laughter peaks.

Under stars that start to twinkle,
The night critters start to sprinkle.
Stories shared beneath the moon,
Nature's fun a bright festoon.

Nature's Aria Beneath the Boughs

Underneath the leafy roof,
A turtle hums a jolly spoof.
Sunlight flickers, bats applaud,
As trees sway like a living squad.

Ducks quack jokes by the stream,
While fish bubble, share their dream.
Frogs croak verses, sweet and sly,
A symphony that can't run dry.

The wind tickles, makes them laugh,
As ants parade, they share a gaffe.
With every rustle, chuckles flow,
In this place where wild things grow.

Beneath boughs, stories intertwine,
A dance of mischief, pure design.
Nature sings in harmony,
A funny world, oh can't you see?

Tones of Timeworn Trunks

Swaying gently, they dance and sway,
Lost in thoughts of yesterday.
Knots and rings tell tales so bold,
Of squirrels that stole treasures of old.

Branches gossip in rustling tunes,
Claiming victory over raccoon swoons.
A woodpecker's tap, oh what a comedian!
Knocking jokes at every occasion.

Breezes giggle through leafy weight,
As shadows play with sticks in gait.
The mossy floor, a carpet of green,
Hosts slow dances, a funny scene.

In this forest, laughter reigns,
With chatter that flows like playful rains.
Roots twist and turn in a jazzy beat,
Making nature's own melody sweet.

Lullabies of the Timbered Realm

In the timbered realm where dreams take flight,
Even owls chuckle at the moonlit night.
Squirrels give concerts, acorn-filled,
As the branches sway, laughter is spilled.

The pines tell stories in a deep voice,
While rabbits leap, as if by choice.
Nature's choir sings not of sorrow,
But jests of joy for a brighter tomorrow.

Twigs snap underfoot, a comedic crunch,
As deer join in for a midday lunch.
Fairies giggle, with mischief displayed,
Planning pranks in the sunlight's cascade.

Leaves shimmy down in spirals of cheer,
While chipmunks perform without any fear.
A lullaby of laughter fills the air,
In the timbered realm, fun is everywhere.

Reflections in the Woodland Whisper

Whispers echo through the leafy walls,
Where laughter and sunlight softly calls.
Frogs croak jokes, quite out of tune,
While ants march on, a miniature croon.

The brook spills secrets with a bubbling glee,
As turtles nod, in a sage decree.
Brambles chuckle at the clumsy hare,
While mushrooms bounce like they just don't care.

Clouds drift by, shaped like silly hats,
Breeze tickles the limbs of lounging cats.
Every rustle a punchline, sharp and bright,
In nature's stand-up, day turns to night.

Dance of shadows, the sun's warm jest,
In this wild theater, we are all guests.
Underneath it all, nature conspires,
To wrap us in giggles by its wild fires.

Chronicles of the Barkbound

In the barkbound tales that twist and twine,
Lies humor that sparkles like sweet wine.
Mice hold court, wearing their best capes,
While the owls poke fun at their silly shapes.

Roots interlock in a tangled game,
Fungi chuckle, shouting names with fame.
Sap drips down like silly tears,
Crafting gigs with whispered cheers.

Bark creaks softly, the tree's wise jest,
While woodpeckers drum with all their zest.
Nature's laughter swells, round and bright,
In the chronicles spun when day meets night.

Conversations bloom where shadows play,
A jigsaw puzzle in the light of day.
In this lively log, comedy won't fade,
For every twist adds a chuckle to the shade.

Swaying to the Forest Rhythms

In the woods, trees twist and shout,
Boughs wave about, there's fun no doubt.
Laughter hangs like leaves so green,
Nature's party, a jolly scene.

Critters dance in leafy shoes,
Squirrels snug in funky hues.
With acorns scattered all around,
They're the dancers, nature's sound.

The sun's a disco ball so bright,
Shining down with pure delight.
Branches sway, they've got the groove,
In this forest, all can move.

So come and join the leafy cheer,
With roots in rhythm, bring your beer!
It's a wild time, but mind your step,
Or you might trip on nature's prep!

The Enchanted Ballad of the Pines

In a glade where pine trees sway,
They gossip in their leafy way.
Whisper tales of bears and moose,
Chasing giggles, what a ruse!

Their needles tickle, oh so sly,
As playful winds go dancing by.
A frog joins in with a ribbit zest,
In this forest, who's the best?

A squirrel strums on twiggy strings,
The joy that nature always brings.
While rabbits hop in cheerful lines,
Together singing, these sweet pines.

Beneath the stars, they laugh and play,
A woodland party, hurray, hooray!
Nature's band in leafy hats,
Join the fun, let's all act like brats!

The Silent Symphony of the Foliage

In the calm where leaves do rustle,
A symphony without a hustle.
Breezes play the flutes so sweet,
While crickets dance on happy feet.

Hush now, listen to the trees,
Making music with such ease.
Inaudible giggles in the air,
A concert that we all can share.

Mice tap dance to hidden beats,
While owls nod in cozy seats.
With every branch that bends and sways,
A silent laugh, amidst the rays.

Underneath the starry skies,
Whispers weave with lullabies.
Nature's joke in every breeze,
Join us, friend, let's laugh with ease!

Reverie Among the Needle-Laden We'll

Amidst the pines, where needles glint,
We gather 'round for laughs, no hint.
The branches bend to hear our jokes,
  As nature winks at merry folks.

Bumblebees buzz in silly tunes,
While raccoons shake their furry moons.
With twigs as microphones we cheer,
  And everyone has come to hear.

Silly squirrels throw leafy hats,
Chasing each other like playful cats.
The forest echoes with our glee,
  In this magical, funny spree.

So let's rejoice 'neath leafy skies,
Join the fun, and let laughter rise!
In this woodland revelry,
  Forever young, wild and free!

Melodies in the Forest Canopy

Squirrels strum on branches high,
While chipmunks dance, oh my, oh my!
A crow's caw is the drummer's beat,
The owls hoot, a rhythm sweet.

The ferns sway in a grassy jig,
A ladybug sports a tiny wig.
Elk stomp their hooves with pride and flair,
Nature's band is beyond compare!

A dandelion wishes it could sing,
But only blows away in spring.
With every gust, a giggle flies,
While butterflies flaunt their big surprise.

In this green stage, the humor flows,
Roots clap along as laughter grows.
Each rustling leaf has a tale to tell,
In timbered joy, we know them well.

The Breath of Silent Giants

Beneath the giants, shadows play,
Where whispering winds hilariously sway.
Their roots are tangled, what a sight,
As critters race, it's a comical fright!

A squirrel falls with acorn might,
Lands on a toad, oh what a fright!
The trees stand tall, they can't help but grin,
Watching fluffballs spin and spin.

With every breeze, there's a giggle shared,
As branches shake, the whole forest stared.
The bark is wise, with stories in jest,
Where laughter echoes, and all are blessed.

Underneath this leafy dome,
The laughter rings, we feel at home.
In nature's playground, joy is found,
And in the silence, fun's all around.

Serenade of the Evergreen

Among the pines, a song takes flight,
As pine cones watch with pure delight.
A skunk does a little dance so fine,
While birds chirp in harmony, just divine.

Each branch swings to a merry tune,
As rabbits hop beneath the moon.
Crickets join with a clatter and cheer,
Serenading the night with no fear.

From silly shadows that prance and sway,
To playful breezes that lead the way.
The humor of life in every frame,
In the evergreen, it's all just a game.

With laughter stitched in bark and leaf,
Nature supplies our sweetest relief.
So join the fun, in daylight's glow,
In this serenade, let laughter flow.

Echoes from the Timbered Heights

In heights where laughter meets the sky,
A parrot squawks a joke, oh my!
With every echo, a giggle sprouts,
As trees conspire, no room for doubts.

A raccoon wears a cap askew,
Looking for snacks, what shall he do?
He finds a peanut, does a quick ballet,
While branches sway, giggling all the way.

Clouds drift by, just like a tease,
While squirrels whisper secrets to the breeze.
Every rustle sparks a chuckle near,
Echoing joy for all to hear.

So in this forest, high and free,
Let laughter roam like a bumblebee.
With every leaf that dances light,
Echoes of joy take joyful flight.

An Anthem of the Timeless Trees

In the forest where they sway,
Trees tell jokes in a leafy way.
A birch laughs, while oaks just chime,
With pines pretending to be sublime.

Squirrels gather for the show,
With acorns flying fast and low.
The roots tap dance, the branches hum,
As tree trunks attempt to drum.

The willow whispers, 'Keep it light!'
While poplars sway with all their might.
Laughter lingers in the breeze,
A woodland comedy that's sure to please.

As sunset glows, they take their bows,
Dancing leaves even get applause!
In this grove of cheeky glee,
Life's a stage for every tree.

Shadows that Sing

In the shadows, crisp and clear,
Frolic creatures come to cheer.
A fox croons with a flashy beat,
While turtles groove on little feet.

Mossy tapestries on the ground,
Breathe with laughter, soft and profound.
With the sun's rays, they play along,
Creating nature's silly song.

Ferns sway gracefully, and then,
Chipmunks jump and shout 'Do it again!'
The breeze jests, tickling the bark,
As shadows dance, igniting a spark.

With a chuckle, the leaves rustle,
The forest joins in this merry bustle.
In this space where fun takes flight,
Shadows sing into the night.

Nature's Symphony in Shade

Under the canopy, where jokes can roam,
The crickets chirp in a rhythmic poem.
Laughter echoes above the glade,
As melodies dance in light and shade.

Cardinals crack jokes from their lofty perch,
Sending giggles down to the birch.
The toad in the pond, quite a croaky chap,
Cackles loudly, 'Well, haven't we got the map?'

A raucous robin, with flair so grand,
Leads the tune with a twinkling band.
The leaves applaud this wild charade,
Creating chants the stars invade.

With every note and playful jest,
Nature's symphony knows no rest.
In the shade, where fun is made,
Life's a concert—let's invade!

The Timeless Choir of the Forest

The trees assemble, quite a sight,
In matching robes, they feel just right.
A chorus of laughter, off-key yet proud,
They fill the woods with their merry sound.

The maple swings her sap, just sweet,
While oaks spread rumor with each hearty beat.
Birches tease the pines for being tall,
As shadows clap, they have a ball.

The crescendo builds, with giggles galore,
A symphony grown from the forest floor.
Even the rocks find their own little groove,
In this timeless choir, they all approve.

As the moon starts to shine their applause is bright,
Echoing through the enchanted night.
Nature's fun with no regret,
Is this the best joke? You bet!

The Language of Leafy Canopies

Under the leaves, whispers rise,
Squirrels gossip, claiming the prize.
A branch bends low, with a creaky sigh,
"Who needs a gym?" a tree calls high.

The acorns tumble, quite a show,
Rolling around like they're in the know.
"Did you hear the one about the stump?"
Heard it all from the beetle's thump.

A breeze blows laughter through the green,
Tickling the trunks, what a scene!
"Life is good," chirps the robins' band,
Dancing on branches, isn't it grand?

And thus they laugh, in sun or storm,
In leafy laughter, they find their form.
A jolly chatter, day and night,
Nature's humor, a pure delight.

Rhythms of Verdant Shadows

In shady places, shadows play,
Where mossy carpets lead the way.
Fungi giggle, as they bloom,
In a giggly room, the forest's loom.

"Hey there, buddy," a fern does say,
"Let's dance around, make the day sway!"
A wily raccoon, in mischief thick,
Sneaks a snack, with his sticky trick.

The sun peeks through in a cheeky beam,
Waking the leaves from a leafy dream.
"Catch me if you can!" they softly tease,
While flipping their ends in the gentle breeze.

And every creature, big and small,
Finds joy in the dance, a whimsical call.
In rhythms of green, they prance with glee,
Turning the forest into a jubilee.

Chants of the Gnarled Firs

The gnarled firs stand, proud and stout,
Chanting tales of what life's about.
With arms wide open, their stories flow,
"Did you know we were all once in a show?"

With bark like wrinkles, they share their jokes,
Tickling the pine cones, cracking the folks.
"Why don't trees play cards?" one asks with glee,
"Too many cheaters, can't you see?"

Brambles giggle, as whispers stray,
While one old fir recalls the play.
"Remember when the wind lost its hat?"
And laughter rolls from the roots to that!

In this wood, where voices blend,
Nature's humor has no end.
With each bough swaying, spirits soar,
Echoing laughter forevermore.

The Echoing Embrace of Trees

In the arms of trees, echoes ring,
Where the birds all gather and sing.
"Watch out!" shouts the owl with a wink,
"Don't step on my branch, or I'll give you a stink!"

The eagles laugh as they soar high,
Plotting their antics under the sky.
"Let's play hide and seek," coos the crow,
"Last one up is a rotten toadstool, oh no!"

With roots that twist and leaves that sway,
They host a party, come what may.
"Who brings the nuts?" asks the old oak keen,
"I promise not to spill any champagne!"

Through every season, the jokes unfold,
In the embrace of trees, we watch tales told.
With chuckles and chirps, they bless the day,
Nature's comedy on display.

Songs Born from the Earth's Veins

In the forest where the squirrels dance,
Frogs croak along, giving life a chance.
Tree branches sway to the tune they hum,
Nature's giggles, oh, what a fun bum!

Pine cones drop like nature's confetti,
And the ground crew is always ready.
Bunnies hop to a beat so sly,
While owls just wink and let time fly.

A ladybug sings a love song loud,
To an audience of a cheerful crowd.
The grass blades sway, it's a wild rave,
"Join us!" they shout, "Be bold and brave!"

So join the fun beneath leafy skies,
Where joy multiplies and laughter flies.
In this orchestra, no need to rehearse,
Just be a tree and embrace the verse!

The Quietude of the Cedar Watchers

In shadows tall, the cedars grin,
With branches crossed, they take it in.
They whisper secrets to the breeze,
While a raccoon sneaks some forest cheese.

Mice gather round for some gossip fun,
"Did you hear what the owls have done?"
They chuckle soft, trying to be sly,
As squirrels scamper, oh my, oh my!

The pines take bets on who will fall,
"Three acorns!" says one, "That's the call!"
With every thud, a party roars,
Who knew falling could open such doors?

In the stillness, laughter grows wild,
Mother Nature grins like a child.
With leafy hats and roots piled high,
These cedar watchers just let life fly!

Echoes of Nature's Serenade

The river sings in bubbly tones,
While frogs hop on their lilypad thrones.
Birds tweet out a fresh morning hit,
Nature's playlist? Never a split!

Branches strum like a guitar well-tuned,
And the flowers sway, all nicely bloomed.
"Dance with me!" calls the dandelion,
While bees buzz by, feeling divine!

The wind tickles leaves into a tune,
Making trees groove beneath the moon.
Every rustle starts to sway the heart,
It's a serenade, a work of art.

In this wild concert of laughter and play,
Nature knows how to brighten the day.
So close your eyes, let your worries go,
Join in the fun, let your spirit flow!

Rhythms of the Tall Guardians

The giant trees tap their sturdy feet,
To every critter's funky beat.
Bouncing squirrels lead the parade,
As shadows dance in nature's glade.

Mighty oaks play the bass so low,
While whispers of wind come in to blow.
"Swing it high! Swing it fast!" they roar,
As forest friends join the uproar.

Branches wave like hands in the air,
While laughter fills the fragrant air.
The sunbeams tap out a radiant beat,
Join this rhythm with happy feet!

Tall guardians, with spirits so bright,
Create joy from morning till night.
Let's celebrate in nature's grand tome,
For this forest is a quirky home!

The Melodic Embrace of Sylvan Spirits

In the woods, a squirrel sings,
Dancing with twigs, on invisible strings.
The rabbits join in, a hopping spree,
While owls hoot loud, 'What about me?'

Frogs croak out their nightly tune,
Mixing with crickets, beneath the moon.
A raccoon laughs, with a mischievous grin,
As the forest party continues to spin.

The trees sway gently, they twist and twirl,
In a leafy dress, they spin and whirl.
With each little gust, they laugh and cheer,
As the woodland revelers gather near.

And when dawn breaks, they fade away,
Leaving behind a light-hearted play.
Even the sun, with a wink and a grin,
Knows that the fun is set to begin!

Resonance of the Tall and True

Beneath tall friends, with bark so grand,
A woodpecker dances, a drummer in band.
The bees are buzzing, they're keeping the beat,
While the hedgehogs tap their tiny little feet.

A bear brings snacks, in a big old sack,
Sharing honey pots, what a tasty knack.
The deer groove in, with elegance and flair,
While the foxes argue about who's more rare.

And when the sun sets, they gather 'round,
For stories and laughter, such joy is found.
With each little pun, and each silly rhyme,
The forest erupts, to the sound of chime.

As stars peek down, they twinkle and glow,
Wondering what wild antics will show.
For in this grove, with spirits so free,
Every night's fun, as fun as can be!

Whispers of the Ancient Woods

In a nook of green, an old tree laughs,
Telling tall tales, of all the mishaps.
With squirrels as actors, and birds the crew,
It's a comedy show, for the brave and the few.

The wind plays a joke, tickles the leaves,
While the raccoon rolls, never believes.
The shadows jiggle, as moonlight peeks,
Making the branches dance, like cheeky freaks.

The porcupine quips, with quills all aglow,
While the hedges giggle, putting on a show.
Each twist is a laugh, each rustle a cheer,
Even the starlight seems to come near.

And as twilight falls, the woods sing loud,
With creatures gathering, feeling quite proud.
For in this enclave, no need for a stage,
Just whispers of joy in this playful age!

Harmony Among the Tall Pines

Beneath the pines, where shadows play,
A hedgehog whirls, brightening the day.
With acorns as maracas, a squirrel will shake,
While turtles come out for a silly break.

The sunbeams join in, with giggles of gold,
Tickling the roots, as stories unfold.
The chipmunks chirp, in a mismatched song,
While the wise old owl looks on, feeling strong.

Each puff of breeze carries laughter so free,
As twigs and branches sway in harmony.
Even the mushrooms join in the fun,
Rolling around, soaking up sun.

At dusk, they settle down, sharing their tales,
Of adventures and mishaps, of storms and gales.
The forest smiles, with glee and delight,
In the embrace of the night, where fun feels just right!

Song of the Evergreen Sentinels

In the woods, the tall ones sway,
Telling jokes in a leafy play.
"Knock, knock!" they whisper with glee,
"Who's there?" Oh, it's just me, the tree!

Roots tickle beneath the ground,
As squirrels giggle all around.
Branches dance in playful tease,
Waving hello to the buzzing bees.

The acorns roll in a game of tag,
While shadows stretch and playfully brag.
"Catch me if you can," they all shout,
As the sun peeks through, brightening the bout.

With a rustle and a chuckle so bold,
The laughter of nature starts to unfold.
When even the wind joins the fun,
You know the frolic has just begun!

Voices Beneath the Canopy

Underneath the leafy dome,
Whispers of mischief find a home.
"Why did the pine cross the road?"
"Because it wanted to lighten the load!"

The branches gossip in a twirl,
Sharing secrets, giving a whirl.
"The willow's weeping? Just a prank!
She's actually got a salty flank!"

Stump the log with a riddle in hand,
"Why are trees so grand, so planned?"
"Because they know how to branch out,
And always have a trunk full of clout!"

Every rustle a laugh, every creak a cheer,
Echoing joy for all who come near.
So find a spot 'neath this green crew,
And join in the fun; there's room for you!

Lullaby of the Whispering Trees

Sleepy branches sway at night,
Telling tales under moonlight.
"Do you know what we've seen today?"
"A chipmunk in pajamas, what a sight to play!"

Night critters chuckle, a merry parade,
As shadows skitter and light invades.
"Why did the leaf join the band?"
"Because it wanted to be a part of the stand!"

Whispers float on a gentle breeze,
While the firs hum tunes just to please.
"Stay up late!" the cedars tease,
"But you might wake the slumbering bees!"

In this realm of giggles and sighs,
Where dreams take root and laughter flies.
A lullaby sweet, a soft, leafy drum,
In the nighttime woods where the jokes aren't dumb!

The Symphony of Green Guardians

Gather 'round, the green brigade,
With laughter, they form a leafy parade.
"Why so serious?" the birch quips bright,
"Let's dance under stars, it'll be a delight!"

The orchestra plays with rustling leaves,
As they tickle acorns while the wind weaves.
"Can you hear that?" the spruce sings proud,
"It's music from nature, clear and loud!"

From the tallest pine to the tiniest sprout,
Each little giggle is what it's about.
Gathering under the twilight sky,
With every note, let your spirits fly!

So join in the fun, under these sentinels,
With joy as pure as the sweet summer bells.
Together we'll laugh, and we'll always be free,
In this merry concert of the green jubilee!

Ballad of the Silent Grove

In a wood where the shadows play,
The squirrels hold court in a fine array.
They chatter and dance, a nutty jest,
While branches above poke fun at the rest.

An owl in a suit thinks he's quite the sage,
But the branches just giggle, turning the page.
The trees lean in close, a gnarled delight,
As they gossip about the moon's silly plight.

The fawns prance in loops, so carefree and spry,
Chasing their tails, oh how they do fly!
While roots pull some pranks on the rocks by the creek,
"Bet you'll never guess what the wind will speak!"

With laughter that echoes, the forest's alive,
Each creature conspires, as they tease and connive.
In this wood full of giggles, harmony reigns,
The jokes of the trees are the sweetest of gains.

Harmonies of the Forest Floor

Underneath where the tall tales grow,
Snails make music in a soft, silent show.
Their shells are the drums, a slow, steady beat,
While ants join in, tapping tiny feet.

A patch of bright mushrooms begins to sway,
With each little wiggle, they dance the day away.
The grass gets jealous, it tries to complain,
But the daisies just laugh and say, "Try again!"

The chattering critters start up a tune,
While worms wriggle by, twirling under the moon.
A concert of giggles from the roots to the sky,
While the breezy old branches hum a lullaby.

So join in the revels on the forest floor,
Where the whispers of laughter ask for nothing more.
In this whimsical realm where humor does soar,
Every creature is welcome to play and explore.

Soliloquy of the Leafy Sky

The leaves gossip high, in a rustling spree,
Each one telling tales, as lively as can be.
"Did you hear of the bird with the wobbly flight?
He thought it was daytime, and it was night!"

A cloud drifts by, with a playful grin,
Jeering at raindrops, "You're late, come on in!"
The sun beams in laughter, glowing with glee,
As shadows engage in a game of hide-and-seek.

Branches wave joy, in a choral display,
While the crows crack jokes, they're the stars of the play.
As wind joins the fun, whistling a tune,
Together they mock the shyness of noon.

Under this leafy quilt, the whimsy is rife,
Nature enacts her own version of life.
So lift your head high, let your heart take a try,
In the giggling green world, you'll never be shy.

The Enchanted Canopy's Tale

Beneath the grand arch of a leafy embrace,
Lies a world full of whimsy, a magical space.
Where owls wear spectacles, reading the trees,
And the chattering squirrels drop acorns with ease.

The foxes recite their most comical lore,
While hedgehogs roll in laughter upon the forest floor.
Each branch is a stage, the sunlight their light,
Where beetles chase shadows, oh what a sight!

The flowers gossip softly, in colors so bright,
"Did you spot the raccoon trying to fly, what a sight!"
While clovers cheer on with a rousing applause,
As nature writes music without any flaws.

So come take a stroll through this charming bazaar,
Where even the silence can laugh, oh so far.
In the enchanted canopy's grand, swirling ballet,
Every leaf becomes part of the playful display.

The Song of Resilient Roots

Beneath the soil they rumble and roll,
Roots twisting and turning, on a quest for a goal.
They hold on tight while the winds do shout,
"Don't pull us up! We're the party turnout!"

With laughter they sway, they've got quite the flair,
Dancing with worms, without a single care.
Who knew their lives were such a hoot?
"Let's dig down deep, let's have a root shoot!"

Their leafy friends above chime in with glee,
"Hey down there, roots! Come up for some tea!"
But roots just chuckle, and one shouts out loud,
"Here's to the depths, we're the underground crowd!"

So next time you wander through forest galore,
Remember the roots, they're the true dance floor.
With laughter and joy, they support every tree,
They're the wild, wacky, deep-rooted jubilee!

Melodies of the Ancient Woods

In the heart of the woods, the trees tell a tale,
Swaying and bending, they never go pale.
With branches a-clapping and leaves full of cheer,
"Come join our jam, it's the best time of year!"

Beneath the tall pines, there's a band made of bark,
They strum on their needles, each note leaves a mark.
Even the squirrels, with their nutty delight,
Join in with their chatter, and dance through the night!

The old oaks reminisce of days gone past,
Speaking in whispers, their stories are vast.
"Remember that storm? What a ruckus it made!
We survived it all, not a single leaf frayed!"

So when you're out roaming, do lend them an ear,
The melodies of woodlands, they're charming and clear.
With laughter and timber, their chorus goes strong,
In the embrace of the ancient, you'll find where you belong!

Harmony in the Green Abyss

Down in the thicket, where shadows do play,
The plants throw a party, it's the green getaway.
Moss chairs set up, and the ferns do the food,
"Join us for fun, it's a leafy green mood!"

With saplings all chatting and vines sharing laughs,
"Did you hear about Wilma? She's grown a few halves!"
Giggling together, as the critters join in,
"Let's tango, let's twist, let our green games begin!"

The daisies and dandelions giggle in rows,
"Look at us swaying, how everybody glows!"
While sunflower hats pass around with great style,
"Dance with us now – just stay for a while!"

So take a pause, let nature's tunes flow,
In the green abyss, with its funny overflow.
Where the joys of the jungle generously thrive,
And laughter surrounds you, keeping the dream alive!

Voices from the Timbered Heights

Atop the tall cliffs where the breezes are bold,
The trees have a summit, where secrets unfold.
"Join us!" they call, with a rustle and sway,
"We're the wise old guards, come hear what we say!"

With a chuckle the maples share stories of yore,
Of critters and breezes that knock at their door.
"Remember the squirrel who thought he could fly?
He jumped from a branch and kissed the sky high!"

The pines join in chorus, their needles a-shine,
"Let's not forget Harry, he loved to recline.
He'd nap all day long in the sun's witty glare,
Then wake up with leaves tangled up in his hair!"

So next time you wander where woodpeckers tap,
Pause to hear gossip, the forest's mishap.
With laughter and wisdom, let the timbered speak,
Their tales will delight you, unique and antique!

www.ingramcontent.com/pod-product-compliance
Lightning Source LLC
Chambersburg PA
CBHW071822160426
43209CB00003B/169